MADE IN CHRIST
160 Powerful Daily Affirmations For Christians

By

Audrey Pearson

"Death and life are in the power of the
tongue and those who love it will eat its
fruits."
Proverbs 18:21

Affirm

I abound in good works.
I have enough to live well and share.
I have in abundance.
I prosper in all things.
I live in good health.

Affirm

I am a savior.
I will succeed and lead.
Together with God, I will see to it that
my dreams are actualized

Affirm

Favour seeks me.
Jobs seek me.
Opportunities seek me.
My labour is fruitful.
The works of my hands are fruitful

Affirm

My needs are met.
My bills are paid.
Nothing and no one gets in my way.
I have the grace for abundance.
I have the power to create wealth.

Affirm

I am productive.
I am prosperous.
My work yields positive results.
I am favoured.

Affirm

Today, I experience ease.
Everything goes smoothly for me.
I don't struggle;
I don't falter.

Affirm

Success is mine.
I'm moving forward.
Everywhere I go I overcome the world.
I am wiser because the wisdom of God is
working in me.

Affirm

My future is bright, brilliant and
beautiful.
It is established in peace, prosperity and
wealth
God's direction is my leading.
This is the life I live.

Affirm

God is my source.
He is my helper.
My finder.
My promoter.
 I walk under an open heaven.
This is a no lack zone.

Affirm

I shine bright.
The lord takes pleasure in me.
He elevates me to the place of honour.
My life is full of light and joy.

Affirm

I have awoken to a surprise.
God has filled my mind with His ideas.
New realms are open to me to conquer.
Purpose inspires me.
God's spirit is a blessing to my life.
My life is a blessing to mankind.

Affirm

Goodness seeks me.
Mercy follows me.
My life is a wonder.
I am powerful in God's will.

Affirm

The spirit of God is my compass.
God will guide my every step.
I am in tune with God's spirit.
I receive all that I need to fulfill my
purpose.

Affirm

I am always led.
Never in the dark, never confused.
God speaks to me
And when he speaks, I hear.

Affirm

I enjoy clarity.
I walk in the light of God.
Navigating life is super easy
Because God walks closely with me.

Affirm

I have God's spirit.
I know the things freely given to me by
God.
I have direction.
I have clarity.

Affirm

My peace is in the will of God.
He restores me;
He strengthens me.
I don't love from a place of fear;
I live by faith.

Affirm

I carry the brand name of God.
Therefore, I live the God kind of life.
My life has meaning.
I live a purposeful life.

Affirm

I unashamedly live for God.
My life proclaims His loving Kindness.
My lips speak of his faithfulness.
My heart shows forth his tenderness.
He is light and because He is in me
I shine to the world.

Affirm

I am divinely blessed.
I am favoured.
Whatever I involve myself in prospers.
I am God's true love.

Affirm

I rise above all things designed to keep
me down.
I trample on my fears.
I live out the liberty I have in Christ
Jesus.
Freedom is my lifestyle.

Affirm

I am of God.
I share His nature.
As He is;
So I am.

Affirm

The life of God is in me.
I am formidable.
I am protected;
Zoe-protected.

Affirm

Because of Jesus, I can do all things.
The works he did, I do also.
Even greater works than he did, I do also.
I move mountains.
There is nothing stopping me.

Affirm

I am anointed;
Powerful in God's will.
Broken free from all bondage.
My faith is in the name of Jesus.

Affirm

I am born of God.
I walk with God.
God works through me to show His power.
He can. So I can.

Affirm

Today,
The words of my mouth are seasoned with
love and grace.
My eyes convey God's love.
My touch brings life to whatever is dead.
My senses are in tune with heavenly
instructions and directions.
I am led by the spirit at all times.

Affirm

I am God's edifice.
Peculiarly designed to emanate his glory.
I am not regular.
I am a different breed.
I am designed for greatness.

Affirm

I am a child of God
And it shows in everything I do.
My words and thoughts are
seasoned with grace.
I live the believer's lifestyle.
I am an active representation of
Jesus Christ on earth.
Glory!

Affirm

I go about dispensing the love of God.
Walking and operating His light!
I do more.
I dare more.
My acts are in line with his will.
I am completely sold out for Christ.

Affirm

I am tightly seated by the Lord's side.
He is my light, hope and joy.
I will hold on to Him in all situations.
I will trust Him even more;
Because I know He loves me.

Affirm

There are no limitations for me.
I set goals and I achieve them.
There is nothing too big for me to do.
I am a child of God and I reign on earth.

Affirm

I am valuable.
I get actively involved in change.
I remain committed to growth and impact.
I live a life of purpose!

Affirm

I am always on God's mind.
He never forgets me,
Never ignores me.
He is mindful of me.

Affirm

I am safe in God's hands;
Wholesomely protected from evil.
He is my shield and shelter,
My love and my father.
He looks out for me all the time.

Affirm

I can do all things
Through Christ who strengthens me!
I depend solely on God and his word.
The word is lamp unto my feet
And a light unto my path.
With the word of God always in my heart
and mouth,
Everything is sure for me!

Affirm

God is with me.
I will not be afraid.
I will not stumble.
I am filled with his love.
My life is made whole.

Affirm

Testimonies upon testimonies.
Victories upon victories.
Good news upon good news.
Upliftment upon upliftments.
Success upon success
This is my reality.

Affirm

This is my season of supernatural growth.
My results are x100
The power of the Lord flows through me.
I am strengthened to fulfill my purpose.

Affirm

The beauty of the Lord is upon me.
I am divinely favoured.
In this season of exponential growth,
I will not miss out.

Affirm

I make the right choices.
The Spirit of God is evident in the steps
I take.
I am divinely directed;
Positioned for eternal success.

Affirm

Grace saved me.
Grace sustains me.
Grace helps me.
Grace builds me.
The grace of God is my daily bread.

Affirm

Today I am reminded of God's word.
I am chosen and loved by God.
I am peculiar; God's special possession.
I have been called into his marvelous
light;
Therefore I act in my new realities.

Affirm

I live a life of enjoyment,
Answered prayers, irreversible blessings,
Open doors, needs met, financial growth
And perfect help.

Affirm

God is working wonders through me.
He is doing a new thing in my life
I am without worry,
Because I serve a faithful God.

Affirm

I am a solution provider.
I am a blessing dispenser.
I am a house of prayer.
I am a Spirit-filled believer.

Affirm

I am empowered to build successful
businesses.
God uses me to creatively solve world
problems.
I am blessed.
I am sponsored by the Holy Spirit.

Affirm

My health has been made perfect.
No sickness, no disease.
I live in good health.
This is the will of God.
This is my reality.

Affirm

I am an expression of God's heart.
I am light.
I have love.
Enriched with all that God gives.
I am guaranteed a great life.

Affirm

I am a winner.
I am a conqueror.
Things align for me.
All things work in my favour.

Affirm

I am named among the great.
Mountains move for me.
I shine like light in my world.
I succeed.

Affirm

I am fully supplied, lacking nothing.
Out of my belly flows rivers of living
water.
I live in plenty.
I live in abundance.
This is my reality!

Affirm

All I do is to the glory of God.
All I am is to the glory of God.
My will, His glory.
My doings, His glory.
My life is a testimony of the glory of God.

Affirm

I am full of grace.
I am full of favour.
I am full of blessings.
I am unstoppable.
I am helped of God.

Affirm

I am constantly moving, constantly
growing.
Constantly evolving.
With God's backing,
 I move at the speed of light.

Affirm

I am God's masterpiece.
Full of His gifts.
I use these gifts to grow the church.
I am in line with God's vision.

Affirm

I am led by the Spirit.
Never in the dark, always in the light.
I am full of ideas, excellence and
innovation.
God's grace is at work in me

Affirm

I am in the era of grace.
I am joyful.
I am favoured.
In this season,
Good things will happen to me.

Affirm

I have joy.
Joy flowing like a river.
Joy deep down in my soul.
The joy of the Holy Spirit is evident in
me.

Affirm

I am helped of God.
Others may fail, I can not.
I am a blessed man/woman.
Fully supplied, lacking nothing.

Affirm

I am a carrier of goodness.
I am a carrier of grace and help.
2022 is my best year yet.
And that's on period!

Affirm

The beauty of God is upon me.
The favour of God is upon me.
I rejoice always.
Never lacking in joy.

Affirm

Everything I lay my hands on,
Turns to pure gold.
Every dream, every idea
Every move I make is inspired by God.

Affirm

The Spirit of the father is within me.
He fills my heart with love.
My heart speaks truth.
The truth has set me free.
 I am free indeed.

Affirm

I am fully helped, fully funded.
All I need is provided.
I am divinely supplied.
Glory!

Affirm

Who am I? A man/woman in Christ.
Where am I? Seated with Christ.
What can I do? All Christ can.
What do I have? All Christ has.

Affirm

I am the stronger one in Christ.
When I show up, evil flees.
I don't avoid evil.
EVIL AVOIDS ME

Affirm

I will pursue.
I will attain.
I will not back down.
I will not give up.

Affirm

I am led by the Spirit.
I take smart and wise decisions,
Because God leads me.
I am forever in the will of God

Affirm

I am a winner in Christ,
So I win always.
 I am a joyful spirit'
So I rejoice always.
In the face of challenges, I rejoice.
NOTHING can take away my Joy.

Affirm

Christ is for me.
Christ is in me.
Christ is with me.
I live by faith.

Affirm

Things work in my hands.
My hands are trained for increase.
I am profitable.
I am full of ideas and innovation.

Affirm

I never forget that I am a child of God.
I never forget my inheritance in Christ.
I never forget the reason for which
Jesus died for me.
I never forget the power I possess as a
result of this.
I never downplay myself.
I am royalty and I live like this.

Affirm

This week,
Only good things happen to me.
I walk in abundance.
I walk in favour.My body is strengthened
with might. There is peace for me.

Affirm

Today, I experience full blown joy.
The type that causes me to laugh out
loud,
To burst out in excitement,
To burst out in thanksgiving,
And to scream, THANK YOU LORD!

Affirm

I am getting better and better.
My faith is working.
My faith is producing.
I have been graciously supplied.

Affirm

Love has changed me.
Love covers me.
I make moves inspired by love.
I am kind, patient, joyful and peaceful.
I dispense love to all around me.

Affirm

I love God because He first loved me.
His love supplies me with Glory.
My eyes have seen the glory of God
My life expresses the Glory of God.

Affirm

I tap into God's love.
He showers me with his love.
This is a no fear zone.
Only faith, always.

Affirm

I am loved.
I am forgiven.
God lives in me.
I experience heaven on earth.

Affirm

I go about today with intent.
I lead a life of integrity.
My thoughts, words, and actions are
honest.
Everything I do, I do out of love.
I live like Jesus. I love like Jesus.
Faith works for me today and always.

Affirm

I am an overcomer.
Challenges have nothing on me.
I am an achiever,
I set goals and I crush them.
I am a victor.
In all ramifications, I win.

Affirm

I am a life giver.
I am a mountain mover.
I am a contending believer.
I am a miracle worker.
This is who I am.

Affirm

I have a good Father.
With him, I lack nothing,
All my needs are met.
All things are working for my good.

Affirm

The goodness of God fills my mouth.
I can taste on my lips.
I can feel it in my heart.
I can see it in all I do.
It is around me.
Take a look at me;
I am a land flowing with milk and honey.

Affirm

My God is a good and loving father.
He cares for, and is intentional about me.
He makes provision for all of my needs.
I have been blessed to be a blessing.
I constantly live out this reality.

Affirm

My mind is at rest.
I will not be troubled.
I am at peace at all times.
I breathe in and breathe out God's peace.

Affirm

The promises of God towards me
Aren't limited to the future
The promises of God towards me are for
now.
I am who God says I am.
Today is full of God's colourful blessings.

Affirm

This is the day that the lord has made.
I will rejoice and be glad in it.
Goodness and favour are my portion.
I am surrounded by God's blessing.

Affirm

I have all that I need to prosper.
God has supplied all I need.
I have nothing to worry over.
God has settled me form life

Affirm

Jesus loves me.
He cares about me.
He will never leave me.
I can trust Him with my life.

Affirm

God is my shield.
He is my exceedingly great reward.
I have God.
I have everything.

Affirm

I am top 1%
I keep getting better and better.
I keep rising.
I keep shining.

Affirm

I am wealthy.
I am healthy.
I am prosperous.
I am rich.
Things work in my hands.

Affirm

Prosperity is in my DNA
I am full of divine leverage.
Full of divine help.
I won in Christ, so I win in life.

Affirm

I am creative.
I am full of ideas.
I am full of ability.
I drip favour.

Affirm

In all things I have the best outcome
possible.
I don't stay down.
I have the blessing.
Heads or tails I win.

Affirm

I can never be poor.
I can never be poor.
I can never be poor.
Again, I can never be poor.

Affirm

I am not pitiable, I am enviable.
I am a fruitful field.
My path overflows with profit.
I'm so blessed, I'm the best in giving.

Affirm

I am more than a conqueror.
I have the best ideas.
I cannot be impoverished.
I will always prosper.

Affirm

God is for me.
He is my great reward
I do not cut corners.
I have Jesus, I have everything.

Affirm

I am the blessed man/woman.
I have the blessing advantage.
I am supernaturally helped.
I live in ease.

Affirm

With faith, I speak these things.
I am whole in all aspects of life.
Career, Family. Finance. Health. Health.
I have all that I need to prosper in life.

Affirm

I am set in the will of God.
I don't chase riches,
Wealth chases me.
God has enriched me.

Affirm

Great things start small.
I patiently sow my seeds and nurture.
Because of God's wisdom, I nurture well
And I reap in folds.

Affirm

I am in my seed phase.
Today I sow.
Tomorrow I reap.
God's wisdom is my fertilizer.

Affirm

I have God's word.
I have a secure future.
His words are YES and AMEN.
His words won't go back to him void.
Therefore, my future is bright.

Affirm

My mind is the seat of God's thinking.
Therefore, my thoughts are resourceful.
My thoughts become my words.
I create my future with my words.

Affirm

I am one with The Most High,
In covenant with The Creator
He is my shield.
What can't touch Jesus cannot touch me.

Affirm

I am not limited by my present
circumstances.
I live in the future where God has
perfected
Everything that concerns me.
I see through God's perspective.
I run with His vision for my life.
Success is guaranteed.

Affirm

I daily renew my mind
I actively guard my soul against negative
influences.
I only see the picture God has painted for
me.
I live out His will.

Affirm

I win the war against negative thinking
patterns.
I see myself as who God has called me to
be.
Things work in my hands.
My growth game is 100%.

Affirm

Totally surrendered, I live God's perfect
will.
Taking the right steps, doing the right
things.
My baby steps become giant strides.

Affirm

I'm a man/woman in Christ.
I live above sin.
I am hidden in Jesus;
Safe and sound from all afflictions.

Affirm

I enjoy favour.
I enjoy rest.
Jesus paid it all.
 I live in abundance.
Nothing missing.
Nothing broken.

Affirm

God is involved in my process.
Leading and stirring me to fruition.
My sowing and sprouting is to God's glory
From seed to sequoia!

Affirm

I am meant to win.
I am meant to rule.
Hence, I thrive.
I win, I rule.

Affirm

I am not afraid.
 If God be for me,
Who can be against me?
I cannot be intimidated.
I am light and life to my world.

Affirm

I hear.
I see.
I know.
I am not ignorant of God's will for my life.

Affirm

God loves me.
He speaks, I hear.
He leads, I follow.
My life is made better for it.

Affirm

Saviors heal. Saviors edify.
Saviors build up
Saviors do not tear down.
I am a savior.
I am light and life in my world.

Affirm

I am bold.
I am courageous.
I am not anxious.
I am not afraid.
 I take over territories.

Affirm

I have clear direction and vision.
I make progress.
I am resilient.
Regardless of difficulty, I keep going!

Affirm

This week, I get more results;
My work ethic gets better.
My creativity gets sharper.
People see the work of my hands and
refer
Me to higher places.
Doors are open for me.
Financially, I flourish

Affirm

Today and always,
My mind is set only on things that are
true.
Things that are noble.
Things that are just.
Things that are lovely.
Things of good report. Things of virtue.
Things that foster praise in my heart.

Affirm

New day, new slate.
God is with me at every point.
He frees me from my fears.
He wins battles I am unaware of.
My life is a beautiful succession of
victories.

Affirm

I welcome this day with outstretched
arms.
Receiving today's dose of God's love.
I have the life of God.
That sweet unending life.

Affirm

I have peace today and always.
He is my God forever.
Guiding me till the end of time.
God is my island hideaway.

Affirm

Nothing shakes me.
Nothing moves me.
I am like a tree planted by water.
I flourish regardless of the situation
around me.

Affirm

Fear has no hold on me.
I make wise decisions.
I think clearly.
I act without bias.
I carry out my civic duties.
And participate in building a great nation.

Affirm

I don't just hear, I speak.
I don't just speak, I do.
I don't just do, I participate.
As I participate, I change the narrative.
My country will be great again.

Affirm

My dreams are not too big.
I am not too small to fulfill them.
I live in an enabling environment
As I work towards my dreams.
I play my part in building a conducive
environment
My country thrives.

Affirm

I rely on Jesus.

I put no confidence in human effort.

I do not dwell on the past.

I look forward only to what lies ahead.

I rejoice in the Lord always.

Affirm

On this blessed day, my steps are
ordered.

I run into progress.

My life makes sense.

This is my moment to shine!

Affirm

I enjoy fellowship with my Father.
I go before Him with boldness.
I patiently listen to what He has to say.
I bask in His love for me.

Affirm

Today I mindfully cast my cares on God.
I trust that He cares for me.
He is able and willing to take care of me.
In this, I rejoice.

Affirm

Today I walk with God.
I find rest in my walk with Him.
Tomorrow, I enjoy the same.
I enjoy rest every single day of my life.

Affirm

This is the day the Lord has made.
I enjoy today.
God is my refuge.
I do not worry about the unknown.
I rejoice and I am always glad!

Affirm

Jesus gets me.
He makes me better. He shows real love
to me.
In this love, I find forgiveness.
I am not condemned. I am saved.

Affirm

Today, my love walk is effective.
People encounter the love of God through
me.
I speak, act and respond with love.

Affirm

I do not have a High Priest who is
Unable to sympathize with my
weaknesses.
Jesus was in all respects tempted as I am
So I will put my trust in him and not in my
ability.
He will keep me from falling.

Affirm

I have been given the ministry of
reconciliation.
I steward this with all faithfulness.
With my words and actions,
I draw men to Christ and not away from
Him.

Affirm

The word of God is my mirror.
The more I look into it,
The more I am transformed into His
image.
I'll keep looking till I become just like
him.

Affirm

I am a new man in Christ.
I am not held back by my old ways.
Christ doesn't care about my past.
My future is bright because;
I am who God says I am.
Loved, redeemed and blessed.

Affirm

Jesus is my role model.
The more I look to Him,
The more I become like Him.
The more I make life changing decisions.
The more my life gets better.

Affirm

I have a very big God.
His love for me is not a fairytale.
He loves me for real
His love never fails.
He is always by my side.

Affirm

Christ defines my identity.
Not the world.
Not my present circumstances.
I am loved, saved, forgiven and freed.

Affirm

I cast my worries on God.
He takes my burden away.
I am not stubborn.
 I let him help me.
Therefore, I enjoy peace.

Affirm

The Holy Spirit is my helper.
I am confident that He is with me.
He will never leave me.
This is my bragging right.
Hence, help is guaranteed.

Affirm

Immanuel!
God is with me.
He lives in me. I live in him.
By all means, He is my rock and fortress.

Affirm

Jesus is my ever present help.
He is my defender.
He is my advocate.
He is my companion.
If He be for me, who can be against me?

Affirm

I have the Spirit of God.
All that I need is in Him.
He has given me EVERYTHING.
I have all I need to live a good life.

Affirm

I have ZOE.
The Spirit of God lives in me.
I enjoy His company every time.
He leads me always.
I can never go astray.

Affirm

God has provided all I need for life.
He has prepared me for a great life.
I walk in boldness.
Nothing stands in my way.

Affirm

I am a man/woman in Christ.
A royal priesthood, a chosen one.
God's special possession.
He has called me into His marvelous light.
By all means, I excel.

Affirm

I have faith.
I am a man/woman of faith.
I think it in my heart.
I speak it with my mouth.
I keep at these till I see my desired
results.

Affirm

I will not give up.
I am destined to overcome the world.
I conquer territories.
At all times, my victory is certain.

Affirm

I live in abundance.
I lay up gold as dust.
I have the wisdom to create wealth.
As I put my God-given wisdom to work,
I am patient for my excellent results.

Affirm

I am not lazy.
I pray. I study.
I read. I learn.
I am not lacking in zeal.
I go about my duties with diligence.
Hence, I stand before kings.

Affirm

Whatever happens
My response is faith over fear
My faith works in every season.
In every situation,
In every economy, I overcome by faith.